THIEVES: MEANING AND TYPES: POLITICAL AND ECONOMIC CAUSES OF STEALING

SAGE

Contents

CHAPTER I

Introduction

A *thief* is a person who steals, especially in secret and without using force or violence.

The plural of *thief* is *thieves.* The related noun *theft* refers to the act or an instance of stealing.

In general, intentionally taking something that doesn't belong to you makes you a *thief.* The word most commonly refers to a person who steals money or physical property, but a *thief* can steal other things, such as ideas, information, or intellectual property.

The word *thief* typically refers to a person who steals without anyone noticing, at least not when the theft is taking place. In contrast, a person who steals by using force, violence, or threats of force or violence would more likely be called a *robber.* Still, the word *thief* is used generally to refer to someone who steals. In this way, a robber is a kind of *thief.*

Most instances of theft are crimes, but a person might still be called a *thief* if they've committed a theft that won't get them arrested.

The first records of the word *thief* come from before the year 900. It comes from the Old English *thēof.*

There is no shortage of ways to be a *thief,* and many of them have a specific name. Some *thieves* steal small things. A petty *thief* is someone who has a record of small thefts. A shoplifter is a *thief* who steals from retail stores. Some *thieves* steal valuable items. Art *thieves*, jewel *thieves,* and car *thieves* are common characters in pop culture. A pickpocket is a *thief* who steals things, such as wallets or watches, directly from people's pockets or from their body.

A burglar is a *thief* who breaks into or otherwise unlawfully enters a home or business to steal valuables. However, while burglars might be called *thieves* in general, this type of theft is more likely to be labeled as *robbery,* since it also involves trespassing on someone's property and invading their space.

CHAPTER II

What is stealing?

Stealing is the act of taking something that doesn't belong to you without permission. When we hear the word "stealing," we often think of someone breaking into our homes or shoplifters trying to smuggle high-priced products out of a store. We think of career criminals, or stealing for dishonest personal gain.

While stealing can be dishonest criminal theft, it can also be the result of poor impulse control or addictive compulsive disorders.

CHAPTER III

Causes of Stealing

Kleptomania

Kleptomania, or compulsive stealing, is a common cause of theft that many forget about. This type of stealing is about a psychological compulsion instead of a desire to profit or gain something material or financial, as defined by the Diagnostic and Statistical Manual of Mental Disorders, 5th Edition.

Kleptomania is a recurrent failure to resist the urge to steal. In most cases of kleptomania, the person steals things that they don't need. The items stolen are often of little to no value, and they could often easily afford the item if they had decided to pay. This is unlike most cases of criminal theft, where items are stolen either out of need or because they're very expensive or valuable.

People with kleptomania feel strong urges to steal, with anxiety, tension, and arousal leading up to the theft and feeling pleasure and relief during the theft. Many kleptomaniacs also feel guilty or remorseful after the act of stealing is over, but are later unable to resist the urge.

People with kleptomania also typically steal spontaneously and alone, while most criminal thefts are planned in advance and may involve another person.

Unlike criminal theft, the items that people with kleptomania steal will rarely be used. They'll likely stash them away, throw them out, or give them to friends and family.

Other causes of stealing

Many other factors besides kleptomania can cause a person to steal. Some people steal as a means to survive due to economic hardship. Others simply enjoy the rush of stealing, or steal to fill an emotional or physical void in their lives.

Stealing may be caused by jealousy, low self-esteem, or peer-pressure. Social issues like feeling excluded or overlooked can also cause stealing. People may steal to prove their independence, to act out against family or friends, or because they don't respect others or themselves.

Risk factors that may cause kleptomania

Different factors can contribute to kleptomania. Genetics and biology may account for a portion of the root causes, which include:

- having other mental illnesses, including bipolar disorder, anxiety disorders, substance use disorders, or personality disorders (The link seems to be strongest with obsessive-compulsive disorder.)
- problems with low levels of serotonin, leading to an increase in impulsive behaviors
- relations with addictive disorders, since stealing can release the rush of dopamine that becomes addictive
- an imbalance in the brain's opioid system, which controls urges
- a family history of kleptomania or addiction
- being female, as two-thirds of people diagnosed with kleptomania are women
- head trauma, like concussions

Psychological trauma, especially trauma at a young age, may also contribute to the development of kleptomania. Family dysfunction can also cause children to steal, which can set the stage for kleptomania tendencies when combined with other mood or addiction disorders.

In children

While parents can find it unsettling, it's not common for young children to steal small things without knowing better. Young children, especially those under the age of 5, are prone to taking things that excite them. When you notice your young toddler or child stealing, you can teach them that it's wrong.

There are a number of reasons older children may steal, and it's rarely out of necessity. Sometimes older children steal as a show of courage or wit, trying to impress peers. In some cases, they'll even do it to act out or get attention.

According to the American Academy of Child & Adolescent Psychiatry, when stealing in older children is persistent, it may indicate behavioral or emotional developmental problems. This can be caused by an unstable home life or genetic factors that can trigger such problems. Children who have consistent issues with stealing often have difficulty trusting others, and may blame the behavior on other people.

In adults

Adults often have very different reasons for stealing than children do. Adults are more likely to steal out of financial need than children. This often makes up a large portion of criminal theft.

Sometimes adults steal out of entitlement. These are often very, very minor thefts, like stealing boxes of tissues or a plush robe (and even mattress pads) from a hotel room, or a stapler from work. The person may feel that they're paying enough for the hotel room, or that they've worked hard enough to have "earned it."

Kleptomania is also a cause of stealing in adults. It causes theft of often small, insignificant items that the person who stole it doesn't need. It's an impulse control disorder, and the person stealing often regrets it immensely after it's over.

Getting help for stealing

When theft is repetitive or is done without any remorse, guilt, or understanding of the impact, it can be a sign of other problems. These can include family trouble, mental health issues, or delinquency. Children who steal often have trouble making and keeping friends, have poor relationships with adults, or have issues with trust.

If emotional or mental health issues could be the reason for stealing, a child might benefit from seeing a therapist or mental health professional.

Treatment for kleptomania

Kleptomania is extremely difficult to treat alone, so getting medical help is a necessity for most who experience it. Treatment typically involves a combination of psychotherapy and medications, which can address triggers and causes.

Cognitive behavioral therapy is most commonly used to treat kleptomania. With this type of treatment, your therapist will help you learn to stop detrimental behavior and address the cognition that causes them. In cognitive therapy, your therapist may use:

- systematic desensitization, in which you practice relaxation techniques to learn to control the urges to steal

- covert sensitization, in which you imagine yourself stealing and then facing negative consequences like being arrested

Medications may be prescribed to address related mood or mental health disorders, like depression or obsessive-compulsive disorder. Your doctor may prescribe a selective serotonin reuptake inhibitor or an addiction medication that balances opioids to balance the brain chemistry that causes the urges to steal.

While kleptomania can't be cured, it can be treated. Continual treatment and caution is required to avoid kleptomaniac relapses. If you've been doing well under treatment and start to experience urges to steal, make an appointment with your therapist or support group as soon as possible.

Identify addiction-related stealing. A kleptomaniac steals merely for the rush and doesn't take the value of the stolen items into consideration. On the contrary, other forms of pathological theft are driven by addiction. In fact, stealing — along with financial difficulties — is often described as one of the warning signs of addiction.

- A person with a substance abuse problem or gambling addiction may take money from relatives, friends, and coworkers to fund their addiction. Lying is also a component of this type of theft; therefore, if the person is confronted about the issue, they are likely to deny having a problem.
- Other signs of addiction may include making friends with a new group while neglecting existing friendships, having trouble with the law, having

difficulty functioning at school and work, and having rocky relationships.

- If you suspect someone you know may be stealing to fund an addiction, get the person professional help immediately. You can approach the person and ask about the behavior: "Lately you've been behaving differently, withdrawing from your friends, and having trouble keeping money. I'm worried you might have a drug problem."
- If the person is in denial about drug use, you can arrange to stage an intervention. An intervention involves other people who care about the person joining you in reaching out to them and explaining your concerns. This can serve as an impetus to get the person into addiction treatment.

Understand that pathological stealing is generally not personal. People who steal pathologically are generally not doing it to intentionally harm anyone. The stealing meets a need — whether emotionally or literally. People who steal for pathological reasons may feel guilty about their behavior, but still be unable to stop it without intervention.

Understand that some people steal to meet their basic needs. Desperation is a common reason behind many thefts. A person may not have a job or source of income or have insufficient means to provide for their family. As a result, the person steals to feed children or provide shelter.

Realize that stealing can happen due to peer pressure. Being in the wrong crowd can also prompt someone to develop a habit of stealing. In such cases, the value of the stolen item may not matter as much as the thrill of taking something and potentially getting away with it. This type of stealing is very common in teens who are susceptible to peer pressure. They may do it to look cool or be accepted by a group of peers.

Notice a lack of empathy. A teenager or person who has difficulty seeing the "bigger picture" may steal without really thinking through their impulsive action might affect someone in the future. The person is not pathological — they are capable of empathy — but in the moment they may act without thinking how stealing will hurt the person or business from which they are stealing. If confronted or asked to think through their actions, this person probably would not steal.

Recognize that some people steal to fill emotional holes. In some cases, a person who has suffered an early attachment loss or trauma may steal to compensate.These individuals' basic emotional needs are not being met. In an attempt to fill an emotional hole left behind by a parent or caregiver, the child may compulsively steal to resolve feelings of deprivation. Unfortunately, the stealing does not resolve the issue, so the individual steals more and more.

Consider that some people steal just because they can. Unfortunately, some thefts occur simply because the person has the opportunity. Maybe they get a sense of excitement from taking what's not theirs. Perhaps they see it as a challenge. They may steal out of greed when they already have plenty.

CHAPTER IV

Types of Thieves

Here are three types of thieves and the best ways to protect yourself against them.

1. The Lazy Thief

The fact is, most thieves are lazy: they will hit easy targets that offer fewer impediments to entry and less chance of being caught, even if that means not getting the biggest "take." Even if a thief can't see expensive items through your windows, but they do see an open window, an easily breakable door or lock, or even evidence that you are out of town, your house may become the preferred target over a wealthier looking house that appears to be more secure.

Lazy thieves are generally less experienced than other thieves, but they are no less serious about their "business." When they enter your home, they will look for expensive items that are easy to carry. They generally won't spend a lot of time in your house because the theft will generally not have been very planned. They probably did not stake-out your property ahead of time. They simply cruised your neighborhood and saw an easy target. Therefore, they will want to get in and out as quickly as possible. These thieves usually target computers, especially laptops, purses and wallets, and smaller electronic equipment.

Combatting this type of thief is pretty much the easiest way to protect yourself from burglary all together because these types of thieves prey on your easy mistakes. The easiest things you can do to protect yourself against these kinds of thieves is quite simple: get deadbolts for all doors (non-deadbolt doors are fairly easy for even inexperienced thieves to get open) and make sure all windows and doors are closed and locked at all times. This may be easy to do during the cold winter months, but when that warm spring weather finally hits, you'll be tempted to let the breeze in. But open and unlocked doors and windows are a huge temptation for lazy thieves.

Of course, doors and ground floor windows are of primary concern. But while ground floor windows are the easiest targets, if someone could reach an open window on a second floor by climbing a tree or using a ladder, it could still offer a tempting entry for a lazy thief. Furthermore, even if you are home, it's really not safe to leave windows and doors open. The last thing you want is for a thief to surprise you in your own home while you are there. Surprised thieves are kind of like surprised wild animals: dangerous. So whether you are at home or out, keep doors and windows closed and locked.

2. The Greedy Thief

The greedy thief is generally a bit more experienced than the lazy thief. Their targets may not be the easiest houses to get into, but the greedy thief knows there is something good inside the house and it's worth breaking in for. Greedy thieves generally target wealthier neighborhoods where they know there will be more expensive things to steal. Usually, these thieves will spend a few days scouting the neighborhood in order to pick a house that will give them the biggest return on their risk.

To avoid becoming a target for a greedy thief, make sure that you move valuables and electronics away from windows so that they cannot be seen from the sidewalk or street. Expensive cars parked in the driveway can also be a tip that there may be expensive goods inside homes. And don't ignore the possibility of a greedy thief just because you don't live in a wealthier neighborhood. If your house gives the impression that there is better stuff to be stolen inside than there is in your neighbors' homes, you could still be a target for a greedy thief.

Greedy thieves generally have a bit more skill and experience than lazy thieves, so while open doors and windows would still be an attraction, you're going to need more than basic safety to protect yourself and your property. The number one thing you can do to protect yourself against a greedy thief is to get a big dog who barks loudly. If a thief approaches a house and hears the sound of a big dog's bark, they are less likely to try to break in.

While a dog can be a great deterrent to greedy thieves, you wouldn't want a thief to harm Fluffy if the thief got inside despite Fluffy's fearsome growl. So whether or not you have a dog, you want something that will protect your home in case an intruder actually gets inside. Your best option for this is a home security system.

There are **three important steps** that raise your level of protection when you have a home security system. **First of all:** arm it! Many people have systems but only use them when they go on vacation or don't use them at all. Home security systems should be set anytime you are away from home and even when you are at home.

Secondly, purchase a system that includes monitoring. A smart thief can recognize the systems that are only alarms and may even know how to get the alarm to turn off once they are inside. Other thieves are so quick that alarm-only units don't even faze them. But a system that provides monitoring will alert you and/or the police as soon as someone breaks in and make it much more likely that the thief will be caught.

Even better, get a system that allows you to view what's going on inside and around your home anytime you want. Many of these systems now have apps that work with your smart phone: you can get alerts on your phone and even view your home from your phone. These features can help police identify thieves, as well.

Thirdly, get signs for your yard or stickers for the windows that announce that your home is protected by a security system. Some people who can't afford entire systems will actually get these signs and stickers without actually getting a system, and that probably does give some thieves a second thought, but we don't recommend advertising a non-existent security system.

Greedy thieves are not as easily deterred as lazy thieves so in order to protect yourself against greedy thieves, you have to not only deter, but also protect. But greedy thieves are not the top of pyramid when it comes to burglary...

3. The Professional Thief

Professional thieves are nearly impossible to deter: if a professional thief decides your property is worth their time, not many of the deterrents we've mentioned will keep them away. They have tried-and-true methods of getting into homes, disabling alarm systems, and quieting barking dogs. So, you need to go the extra step to protect you, your family, and your home from a professional thief.

Professional thieves will generally stake-out their targets well in advance of performing the burglary. They will know your daily pattern: when you go to work, when you walk the dog, when you mow the lawn (all opportune times to commit a burglary), etc. If possible, vary your daily routine as much as possible. The vast majority of thieves would rather not run into you inside your home so not being able to figure out when you're home and when you're away will be a good deterrent.

Many thieves will have gained access to your home, innocuously, prior to the break-in. If you are having work done in your home and have to give the company a key to your home, you should always change all the locks after the work is finished, even if the key is returned. You don't know who had access to the key; they could have copied it and could be planning to come back months later and be able to walk right in your front door.

But changing all your locks even once or twice a year can be a pain and of course costs money every time you do it. One excellent way to avoid this problem is to purchase a keyless entry system. With an up-to-date keyless entry system, you will be able to have multiple user codes and you will be able to delete or add user codes easily. So, you can offer service people a code made just for them in order to get into your house and then you can delete the code once the work is complete. Many of these systems record attempts to access your home, so you can even check to see if someone tried to use a deleted code.

Since professional thieves usually know how to disable video monitoring equipment, let them. Wait, what? That's right – let them think they're disabling your monitoring system. Have cameras visible on the exterior of your home, and perhaps a few inside, but have another system that uses hidden cameras. Technological advances mean you can get security cameras that are quite small and undetectable, especially if a thief isn't looking for them. If a thief disables a few cameras and even an alarm system, they will think they are set and they won't be looking for more monitoring equipment. So, outsmart them by having a faux system on top of your real system.

If you have very valuable items or large amounts of cash in your home, consider taking steps to protect those items. A large, heavy safe can keep items that are not routinely used secure. Small tracking devises can also be purchased for high value art and furniture pieces and even electronic equipment.

In short: if you want to protect yourself from the most clever and determined of thieves, you need to take every advantage technology can offer you.

CHAPTER V

Political Causes of Thief

The following is a list of some of the most common political crimes and a short description of each.

Bribery is the act of giving money or assets to a political figure in exchange for that person to vote or speak on behalf of a certain law or belief system. This is a crime because the political figure is doing this for their own gain, and not for their own personal ideals or to benefit the citizens of the state.

Treason is when a person does something to deliberately betray their country. This could be anything from the murder of a political figure to leaking state secrets to another country.

Sedition is the process of getting a group of people impassioned to create a revolution against their own government.

Espionage occurs when a country or group uses individuals to spy on the government and report back.

Theft can vary as a political crime, but it can be a political figure stealing money from the government or even stealing money from groups and activists.

Perjury is lying under oath, but it is a political crime if an individual is caught lying under oath to wrongfully convict a political figure or cause unrest within the government.

Politics and Crime

Politics and crime unfortunately have been connected dating all the way back to the days of tribal leadership. A **political crime** is any crime that is judged to have been committed in order to harm the state, state's government, or political system of a state. This means that a crime committed by a politician is not necessarily a political crime. If a governor decides to assault his wife, he will have committed the crime of domestic abuse. However, if the same governor takes a bribe to advocate for a law to benefit a large corporation, then it would be considered a political crime.

This means that although violence can be part of political crimes, they can be non-violent in nature. Although the United States does not have a crime category that pertains solely to political crimes, they have occurred in the past, and individuals continue to be prosecuted and convicted. The accused may believe that something needs to happen that can only be done with manipulation or are afraid for their nation, so they are willing to commit a crime in order to protect it in their mind. Despite the criminal's best intentions, these actions are still illegal and are punished with varying severity; instead of categorizing the crimes under a broad header, they are dealt with on an individual basis.

CHAPTER VI

Economic Causes of Thief

Possible causes for acts of theft include both economic and non-economic motivations. For example, an act of theft may be a response to the offender's feelings of anger, grief, depression, anxiety and compulsion, boredom, power and control issues, low self-esteem, a sense of entitlement, an effort to conform or fit in with a peer group, or rebellion. Theft from work may be attributed to factors that include greed, perceptions of economic need, support of a drug addiction, a response to or revenge for work-related issues, rationalization that the act is not actually one of stealing, response to opportunistic temptation, or the same emotional issues that may be involved in any other act of theft.

The most common reasons for shoplifting include participation in an organized shoplifting ring, opportunistic theft, compulsive acts of theft, thrill-seeking, and theft due to need. Studies focusing on shoplifting by teenagers suggest that minors shoplift for reasons including the novelty of the experience, peer pressure, the desire to obtain goods that a minor cannot legally purchase, and for economic reasons, as well as self-indulgence and rebellion against parents.

CHAPTER VII

Conclusion

There are various reasons why people steal. It may be as a result of several problems like economic, political, social and so on.